S0-BAI-315

Countries of the World

Peru

by Kristin Thoennes

Consultant:
Juan Del Campo
First Secretary, Information Officer
Embassy of Peru in the U.S.A.

Bridgestone Books

an imprint of Capstone Press
Mankato, Minnesota

Bridgestone Books are published by Capstone Press
151 Good Counsel Drive, P.O. Box 669, Mankato, Minnesota, 56002
www.capstonepub.com

Copyright © 1999 by Capstone Press, a Capstone imprint. All rights reserved.
No part of this book may be reproduced without written permission from the publisher.
The publisher takes no responsibility for the use of any of the materials
or methods described in this book, nor for the products thereof.
Printed in the United States of America in Stevens Point, Wisconsin.
042011
006165

Library of Congress Cataloging-in-Publication Data
Thoennes, Kristin.
    Peru/by Kristin Thoennes.
    p. cm.—(Countries of the world)
    Includes bibliographical references and index.
    Summary: Presents the landscape, culture, food, animals, and sports of Peru.
    ISBN-13: 978-0-7368-0155-3 (hardcover)
    ISBN-10: 0-7368-0155-3 (hardcover)
    ISBN-13: 978-0-7368-8380-1 (paperback)
    ISBN-10: 0-7368-8380-0 (paperback)
    1. Peru—Juvenile literature. [1. Peru.] I. Title. II. Series: Countries of the world (Mankato, Minn.)
    F3408.5.T46 1999
    985—dc21   98-41778
                                                                                   CIP
                                                                                    AC

Editorial Credits
Blanche R. Bolland, editor; Timothy Halldin, cover designer; Linda Clavel and Steve Christensen,
    illustrators; Kimberly Danger and Sheri Gosewisch, photo researchers

Photo Credits
Images International/Erwin C. "Bud" Nielsen, 18
Jerry Ruff, 5 (bottom)
Michele Burgess, cover, 6, 16
Ren Navez, 8
StockHaus Limited, 5 (top)
Tom Stack & Associates/Inga Spence, 14; Tim O'Keefe, 20
Victor Englebert, 10, 12

Table of Contents

Fast Facts

Name: Republic of Peru

Capital: Lima

Population: About 26 million

Languages: Spanish, Quechua

Religion: Mostly Roman Catholic

Size: 496,222 square miles (1,285,215 square kilometers)

Peru is almost the same size as the U.S. state of Alaska.

Crops: Cotton, sugarcane, coffee

Maps

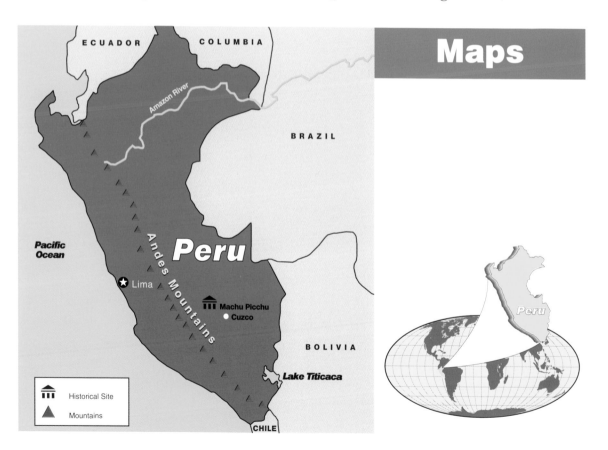

Flag

Peru's flag has three equal vertical stripes. A white stripe lies between two red stripes. A shield is in the center of the white stripe. The llama on the shield stands for Peru's animal life. The tree stands for Peru's plant life. The horn of plenty filled with gold coins represents Peru's mineral wealth.

Currency

The unit of currency in Peru is the nuevo sol. One nuevo sol consists of 100 centimos.

In the late 1990s, about 3 nuevos soles equaled 1 U.S. dollar. About 2 nuevos soles equaled 1 Canadian dollar.

The Land

Peru is a country of mountains and forests in western South America. The Pacific Ocean borders Peru's long western coastline.

Three types of land cover Peru. A narrow plain lies along the coast. Very little rain falls in this area. Most of Peru's cities are on the coast.

The highlands are in the middle of Peru. This area includes the Andes Mountains. The Andes is the world's second-highest mountain range. The long Amazon River begins in the Andes.

The lowlands make up eastern Peru. Many rivers flow through this region. Travelers use rivers instead of roads. Thick rain forests cover the lowlands. Few people live in this hot, rainy area.

Most of Peru is too dry, steep, or wet for farming. Peruvians farm only about 2 percent of the land. The Incas were the first people in Peru. They built steplike terraces to farm on mountains.

The Incas farmed on terraces at Machu Picchu.

The People

Three main groups of people live in Peru. Almost half the country's people are native Peruvians. More than one-third of Peruvians are mestizos (mess-TEE-zos). They are part native Peruvian and part European. Most of the other people in Peru have European backgrounds.

About 70 percent of Peruvians live in cities. Some people live in apartments there. Others have houses with patios. Peruvians often eat and rest on these paved, outdoor areas.

Most families in the countryside live in small houses. Many homes do not have running water or electricity. Peruvians who live near the Amazon River build their homes on stilts. These houses stand high above the ground to stay dry. People who live near Lake Titicaca (ti-ti-KAH-kah) build houses and boats from tortora reeds. These hollow grasses grow in the lake.

Lake Titicaca houses and boats are made of reeds.

Going to School

Peruvian children attend school from ages 6 to 16. Grade school lasts six years. Five years of secondary school follow. Children must attend both primary and secondary school.

Peruvian students take science, math, and Spanish classes. They also study writing, history, and English. Other classes might include music, art, and physical education.

Peru has both public and private schools. The government runs public schools. They are free. Private schools charge money. Some of these schools are religious schools run by the Roman Catholic church.

Some children in Peru cannot attend school. The country does not have enough teachers or schools. The government is building small schools in places where few people live. These nucleos (NOO-klee-ohs) often have only one room.

Most children in Peru wear uniforms to school.

Peruvian Food

The most important foods in Peru are potatoes, peppers, and rice. Hundreds of kinds of potatoes grow in Peru. Native Peruvians probably were the first people to plant potatoes.

Piqueo (pee-KAY-oh) are foods that people eat before the main meal. Peruvian piqueo are very filling. A favorite piqueo consists of sliced potatoes with a spicy peanut and cheese sauce.

Hot peppers make Peruvian food spicy. Peruvians near the sea eat peppers with fish. Many highland Peruvians like extra-hot peppers. People in the rain forest enjoy vegetables with hot pepper dip.

Peruvians who live by the sea often eat fish. Ceviche (sah-VEE-chay) is a popular seafood dish. Lime juice and spices flavor the raw fish in ceviche. Some Peruvians eat vegetables instead of fish or meat. Corn on the cob is a favorite vegetable.

Peruvians grow and sell many kinds of potatoes.

Clothing

The type of clothes Peruvians wear depends on where they live. People in cities wear clothes like people wear in North America. Farmers in the highlands dress in traditional clothing.

Women in the highlands wear full skirts called polleras (po-YEH-rahs). Women wrap mantas (MAHN-tahs) around their shoulders. These large cloths are brightly colored.

Men in the highlands wear loose shirts and black pants. Many men also wear vests.

Both Peruvian men and women often wear hats. Monteras (mon-TEH-rahs) have brims to provide shade from the sun. Some men wear chullos (CHOO-yohs). These caps cover the ears.

Ponchos (PON-chohz) keep people in the highlands dry and warm. A poncho is a blanket with a hole that fits over the head.

Women wear polleras and mantas.

Animals

Three animals in Peru look like small camels without humps. Llamas are very common in Peru. They carry goods. The vicuña (vi-KYU-nya) and alpaca have finer wool. Peruvians use llama, vicuña, and alpaca wool for clothes.

Many animals live in the Andes Mountains. Andean foxes get their name from these mountains. Mountain lions and deer also roam the Andes.

The thick forests of the lowlands provide homes for many other animals. Monkeys and jaguars hide among the trees. Snakes crawl through the thick grass. Alligators and piranhas swim in the region's many rivers.

More kinds of birds live in Peru than in any other country. Peru's most famous bird is the Andean condor. It has a wingspan of up to 10 feet (3 meters). Colorful parrots nest in the lowland rain forests. Flamingos live near the water.

Llamas carry goods and provide wool for Peruvians.

Sports and Games

Peruvians play some of the same sports as North Americans. Soccer is Peru's most popular sport. Both children and adults play soccer. Peruvians also enjoy playing basketball and volleyball.

Bullfighting is very popular in Peru. The bullfighting season lasts from October through December. In a bullfight, matadors wave red cloths to tease bulls. These bullfighters sometimes ride a horse. The fight ends when the bull dies.

Many Peruvians enjoy watching cockfights. Trained chickens with sharp spurs on their legs fight each other.

Sapo is a popular game in Peru. Players place a metal toad on a table. They try to throw game pieces into the toad's mouth. Peruvians often play sapo in restaurants.

Soccer is a popular sport throughout Peru.

Holidays and Festivals

Peruvians take time out for fun at fiestas. Fiesta (fee-EST-a) is the Spanish word for festival. Nearly all towns in Peru have their own Catholic saint. On the saint's day, church bells ring. Peruvians celebrate with fireworks and parades.

Carnavales (kar-nah-VAH-lays) is a party before Lent. Carnavales lasts three days and three nights. People dress in costumes and masks. They dance, eat, and drink.

Inti Raymi (EEN-tee RYE-mee) was a special day for the Incas. These early Peruvians honored the sun. Inti Raymi means Festival of the Sun. Many native Peruvians still celebrate Inti Raymi. They burn fires all night on the longest night of the year. They pray for the sun to return.

Independence Days in Peru are July 28 and 29. These days are a time for speeches and military parades.

Many native Peruvians still celebrate Inti Raymi.

Hands On: Make a Terrace

The Incas formed flat platforms of land on mountain slopes in Peru. These terraces allowed Incas to farm steep land. You can make a terrace model.

What You Need
Clay
Table knife
Stones

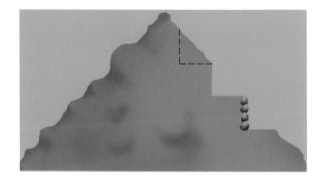

What You Do
1. Form the clay into a mountain with your hands.
2. Start near the bottom of the mountain. Make a line with the knife across one side of the mountain. Trace another line about 1 inch (2.5 centimeters) higher.
3. With the knife, cut in at the lower line. Cut down at the upper line until you reach the first cut. Push out with the knife to remove the clay between the two lines. This will form the first step of the terrace.
4. Put stones in the terrace wall. This will help to hold the clay in place. Repeat steps 2-4 farther up the clay mountain.

Learn to Speak Quechua

father	taita	(TYE-tah)
mother	mama	(MAH-mah)
no	mana	(MAH-nah)
please	ama jina kaychu	(AH-mah JEE-nah KAY-choo)
thank you	taitacha pagasunki	(tay-TAH-chah pah-gah-SOON-kee)
yes	ari	

Words to Know

Lent (LENT)—the 40 days before Easter in the Christian church's year

nucleo (NOO-klay-oh)—a small country school started by Peru's government

patio (PAT-ee-oh)—a paved area next to a house; people use patios for relaxing or eating outdoors.

piranha (puh-RAW-nah)—a flesh-eating fish with very sharp teeth

poncho (PON-choh)—a blanket with a hole in the center that fits over the head; South Americans were the first people to wear ponchos.

Read More

Allard, Denise. *Postcards from Peru.* Austin, Texas: Raintree Steck-Vaughn, 1997.

Landau, Elaine. *Peru.* A True Book. New York: Children's Press, 2000.

Internet Sites

FactHound offers a safe, fun way to find Internet sites related to this book. All of the sites on FactHound have been researched by our staff.

Here's all you do:

Visit *www.facthound.com*

Type in this code: 0736801553

Index